Snap books™

Cheerleading

Cheer Spirit

Revving Up the Crowd

by Jen Jones

Capstone press

Mankato, Minnesota

Snap Books are published by Capstone Press,
151 Good Counsel Drive, P.O. Box 669, Mankato, Minnesota 56002
www.capstonepress.com

Library of Congress Cataloging-in-Publication Data
Jones, Jen, 1976-
  Cheer spirit: revving up the crowd / by Jen Jones.
    p. cm. — (Snap books cheerleading)
  Includes index.
  ISBN 0-7368-4362-0 (hardcover)
  1. Cheerleading — Juvenile literature. I. Title. II. Series.
  LB3635.J64 2006
  791.6'4 — dc22   2005007268

Summary: A guide for children and pre-teens on building team and crowd
spirit through cheerleading.

Editor: Deb Berry/Bill SMITH STUDIO
Illustrators: Lisa Parett; Roxanne Daner, Marina Terletsky and Brock Waldron/Bill SMITH STUDIO
Designers: Marina Terletsky, and Brock Waldron/Bill SMITH STUDIO
Photo Researcher: Iris Wong/Bill SMITH STUDIO

Photo Credits: Cover: Tim Jackson Photography; 4, Bettmann/Corbis;
8, The Image Bank/Getty Images; 11, (r)Comstock Images/Getty Images
12, The Image Bank/Getty Images; 18, Les Stone/Corbis; 20, Paul Barton/Corbis; 22, BananaStock Ltd.;
26, Corbis/Phil Schermeister; 28, Paul A. Souders/Corbis; 32, Britton Lenahan. Back Cover, Getty Images.
All other photos by Tim Jackson Photography.

1 2 3 4 5 6 10 09 08 07 06 05

Table of Contents

Catch the Cheer Spirit

In the early days of cheerleading, men with megaphones simply yelled their "Rah, rah, rahs!" Modern cheerleading has become an exciting athletic activity that involves men and women. Though much has changed over the decades, one thread runs throughout. School spirit.

Raising school spirit is the main duty of a cheer **squad**. (No wonder cheerleaders were once called "spirit leaders.") Spreading school spirit creates student unity and shows your sports teams that they have a lot of support. Throughout this book, you'll learn about:

▶ Winning attitudes
▶ Making pep rallies fun and memorable
▶ Dos and don'ts for getting the crowd involved
▶ Ways to boost school and team spirit
▶ Why spirit is so important in cheerleading

At pep rallies, games, and even during school, you'll have plenty of opportunity to spread the spirit. Remember that cheerleading is a lifestyle. When you sign on to the squad, you sign on to be a spirit leader. Take your responsibility seriously. After all, spirit starts with you!

"Spread the spirit!"

SPREADING SPIRIT

Winning Attitudes

Excitement. Joy. Energy. As a cheerleader, you have the power to make the crowd feel these things. During games, the fans look to the squad for direction and entertainment. To be a good spirit role model, you must always display good **sportsmanship** and **showmanship**.

" Spirit starts with you! "

Sportsmanship means losing gracefully, playing fairly, and treating others with respect, especially the opposing team. Teasing or being rude to other teams isn't classy. Give your school a good name.

Showmanship describes your performance style. Do you enjoy being in front of the crowd? Does your face show excitement and happiness? Imagine watching a play where all of the actors spoke in a flat voice. You'd probably fall asleep! The same rules apply in cheerleading. If you enjoy yourself while performing, the crowd is likely to enjoy watching you.

Always keep these two "S" words in mind and you'll be on the right track to a winning attitude.

Revving Up the Crowd

For a cheerleader, there's nothing worse than staring out at a sea of bored faces. When a sports team is having a so-so season, it can be a chore to rev up the crowd. Try these surefire pointers to give your school a spirit lift.

Bribe them with goodies

Freebies like T-shirts and mini-footballs will bring a smile to any fan's face! During halftime and time-outs, offer the items as rewards for good spirit. Arm your squad with slingshots and fire away toward the loudest fan section.

Stir excitement with a run-through

At the beginning of a game, some teams do a "run-through" when introduced. When the team name is announced, the football players burst through a giant banner made by the cheerleading squad. The banner can feature encouraging phrases like, "Tame the Titans!" Seeing the football team so pumped up is a can't-miss way to pump up the crowd.

FiRST TEAM!

Need more spirit boosters? Try these on for size.

Let the music play Dance numbers are always fun and exciting for the crowd. Use songs like *We Will Rock You* or *Are You Ready to Rumble?* as a starting point. Soon the crowd will be singing a new tune!

Bring on the noise Pass out noisemakers or cowbells to the crowds. Signal for fans to ring the bells whenever the team scores. Cowbell noise can also add fun and excitement before the game starts.

Pump it up with props Use signs to lead the crowd in simple chants. For instance, the left section yells, "Go," and the right section yells, "Tigers!" Soon your dull roar will be the roar heard 'round the world!

Go for the gimmicks Invite junior cheerleaders to perform at halftime. If you're on a squad with boys *and* girls, come up with a funny guys-only routine. Fun, new ideas are everything!

From Our Team to Yours

Whether your sports teams are on a winning streak or in a losing slump, they need encouragement! Though it might feel like the players don't notice your squad on the sidelines, chances are they appreciate your support more than you know.

Candy Elves

Surprise the athletes with candy bags and encouraging notes. The sweet treats and kind words will put big smiles on the players' faces.

Locker Room Surprise

Sneak into the locker room and decorate it before the big game.

Sea of Signs

Before games, each cheerleader should make at least ten signs to hang around the school. Decorate with sayings like "Bring it Home, Tigers" using colorful markers.

These ideas will improve not only team spirit, but also relations between your team and theirs. Who knows? You might just find those athletes, who seemed like they didn't care, supporting your squad at competitions!

Pep Rally Pizzazz

For a very long time, pep rallies have been a treasured tradition. Some schools hold bonfires while others meet in the gym. But they all have the same goal of spurring the team to victory. Guess who is at the center of every pep rally? The cheerleaders!

Games, skits, and cheers get the crowd involved and fired up. Look through our pep rally idea bin and see what you think will be fun.

Games

Pit the classes against each other or go for "boys against girls." After you've got teams, have a blast with games like these.

Half-Court Shot Select someone from each class to go for the half-court gold. The winning class gets bragging rights and the best seats at the game!

Sore Throat City The team that sends the "noise meter" off the charts gets free admission to the game.

Olympic Gold Light the spirit torch with a mini-Olympics! Classmates compete in events like tug-of-war and "Pin the Tail on the **Mascot**."

Skits

Skits are a fun way to rope teachers and athletes into taking part in the pep rally. Students will love seeing their math teacher in costume or the quarterback in a cheer uniform. Anything goes! Are you stuck for skit ideas? Use these as a starting point.

The Dating Game

A wall separates a cheerleader from three possible dates: your team mascot, the opposing team mascot, and Cupid. The cheerleader asks funny questions to determine who's a match. Your mascot wins!

Freaky Friday

After a freak accident, a cheerleader and teacher switch identities. The teacher performs with other school staff in full uniform, while the cheerleader "teaches" the crowd the winning game strategy.

The Bottom Line

Plan to perform several cheers and dances. Figure out a schedule beforehand (such as opening cheer, skit, game, dance, coach's speech, etc.) Songs like *Another One Bites the Dust* are sure to get everyone on their feet. When everyone takes part, you know your pep rally is a success!

Game Time

Whether in the freezing cold of football or the high-speed action of basketball, the game atmosphere is like no other! While the team provides the main attraction, your squad raises the fan experience.

Ideas for game time greatness

Every time the team scores a touchdown, your squad does push-ups equal to the amount of the score. The crowd counts out loud as you go. (Added bonus, you'll be buff if you're cheering for a high-scoring team!)

Every time the team scores, your cheer captain runs with the team flag around the track or the court!

Give the cheering section a catchy name like "Cougar Crazies" or "Bleacher Creatures."

Decide on a team signature stunt, such as a basket toss after every touchdown or a shoulder stand during a victory chant.

To spread spirit to the other team, take time to go over to the other side and perform a "Good Luck" or "Welcome" cheer.

19

Theme Week Fun

School spirit reaches a peak at yearly events like Homecoming and Spring Fling. This is the time when students, school staff, and alumni let their hair down! To add fun to the events, your squad can have a "Spirit Week."

During Spirit Week, have a dress-up day challenge. For instance, Monday could be "Wig Day," Tuesday "Hawaiian Day," Wednesday "Backwards Day," Thursday "Oldies Day," and Friday "Team Day." Every day, each class picks the person with the best outfit to compete at the pep rally. Everyone will have a blast with this activity!

Voting activities such as "Best Eyes" or "Cutest Baby Picture" are also popular theme week ideas. Set up a table in the lobby as a voting station with pictures of the homecoming court or cheer squad. (Keep secret who is shown in each picture.) Students vote by putting money in the jar next to their favorite picture. Money goes into the squad budget or to charity.

Keeping Spirits Up on the Squad

Whew! As a year-round sport, cheering can be energy-draining. That's why it's just as important to keep squad spirits up as it is to raise school spirit.

To be your best, you need to be well rested, healthy, and happy. If you ever get exhausted, talk to a teammate or coach about your feelings. Take a deep breath and remember that your well-being comes first.

Sometimes there may be tense moments on the squad. When people have different ideas or spend a lot of time together, it's normal to have raw nerves. The key is addressing problems with your coach, who can work out any issues that may arise. Communication is the key.

Team-building activities and get-to-know-you games can help strengthen bonds between teammates. These games can be done during practice or at squad retreats. Your squad works hard! Take time out to relax by having sleepovers or movie nights.

Earning the Treasured Spirit Stick

The spirit stick earned its place in cheer history after being featured in *Bring It On!* In case you've been hiding under a rock and don't know what it is, we'll clue you in.

Spirit sticks are awards given to the most spirited squads at cheer camp. Legend says that if your spirit stick touches the ground, your squad will be cursed forever. (Think of the legend this way, if you always keep your spirit up, your squad won't have any problems!)

Though four days of camp can be exhausting, try to keep your energy high. The instructors are on the lookout for squads who show good attitude and purpose. Increase your spirit stick chances with these tips.

▶ If teams break out in chants during breaks, don't be the squad that is "too cool for school." Join in!

▶ Don't let **competition** come between possible friendships with other teams.

▶ Show up on time to classes and events. Pay attention and show interest in learning the material.

Follow these rules and you'll soon have a shiny spirit stick lining your trophy case!

"Keep your energy high!"

Honoring the Fans

Build spirit by rewarding the biggest fans for their support! Here are some easy ways to recognize loyal game attendance.

Honor different groups at every game

For instance, "Freshman Night" could encourage your school's new students to show their faces in the stands. "Team Alumni" nights put the spotlight on past players. On their special night, each group receives a shout-out, welcome signs, and team goodies.

Select a "Number One Fan!"

This person can range from an adult fan who never misses a game to a tiny tot bursting with energy. Winner gets a "Fun Fan Makeover" at halftime, complete with face paint and pom-poms!

Give fans something to remember the game

Tape a raffle ticket underneath five chairs in the cheering section. At halftime, tell fans to check their seats. Lucky winners get season passes!

Singling out the most super fans will show your team's supporters that they're appreciated. The result? They'll keep coming to games! Everyone wins.

"Put the spotlight on!"

You Don't Mess with Tradition

Tradition is the stuff sports teams are made of. Your school's fight song, mascot, and alma mater are all part of a rich tradition that should not be ignored. Include these old stand-bys in your squad's routines and keep them alive.

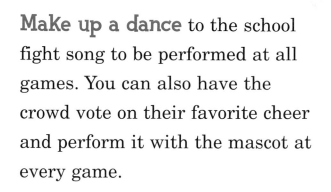

Make up a dance to the school fight song to be performed at all games. You can also have the crowd vote on their favorite cheer and perform it with the mascot at every game.

Create a hand signal for the crowd in the shape of a letter, horns, a #1. You get the picture! Throw the signal after every score or as support before an important play.

Don't forget special squad traditions, such as wearing your warm-ups to school every Friday or doing a special chant privately before games. The traditions you start today will be passed on to your school's cheer squads of tomorrow. Leave a lasting mark!

GLOSSARY

alma mater (AWL-ma-MAW-tur) a school from which someone has graduated

alumni (uh-LUM-nye) people who have graduated from or attended a school

competition (kom-puh-TISH-uhn) a contest where two or more people are trying to win the same thing

mascot (MASS-kot) a symbol of a sports team believed to bring good luck

megaphone (MEG-uh-fone) a cone-shaped device used to make your yells louder

showmanship (SHOH-muhn-ship) letting the audience know you enjoy performing through your attitude

sportsmanship (SPORTS-muhn-ship) treating other teams with respect and fairness

squad (SKWAHD) a team of cheerleaders

tradition (truh-DISH-uhn) a practice that is carried on through the years

FAST FACTS

It's All Greek to Me

Megaphones are believed to have come from ancient Greece, where actors wore megaphone masks that made their voices sound louder for the crowd.

Pep in Your Step

In 1919, the first-ever pep rally was held at the University of Kansas to raise money for a new sports stadium.

A Spirit Stick Is Born

Pom-pom inventor George Herkimer definitely had spirit to spare. To reward a team at one of his cheer camps, he painted a twig and presented it to the cheerleaders as a reward. That day, spirit sticks were born!

READ MORE

Golden, Suzi J. and Roger Schreiber. *101 Best Cheers: How to Be the Best Cheerleader Ever*. New York: Troll Communications, 2001.

McElroy, James T. *We've Got Spirit: The Life and Times of America's Greatest Cheerleading Team*. New York: Berkley Publishing Group, 2000.

Neil, Randy and Elaine Hart. *The Official Cheerleader's Handbook*. New York: Fireside, 1986.

Peters, Craig. *Competitive Cheerleading*. Broomall, Pennsylvania: Mason Crest, 2003.

Wilson, Leslie. *The Ultimate Guide to Cheerleading*. New York: Three Rivers Press, 2003.

INTERNET SITES

FactHound offers a safe, fun way to find Internet sites related to this book. All of the sites on FactHound have been researched by our staff.

Here's how

1. Visit *www.facthound.com*
2. Type in this special code **0736843620** for age-appropriate sites. Or enter a search word related to this book for a more general search.
3. Click on the **Fetch It** button. FactHound will fetch the best sites for you!

ABOUT THE AUTHOR

While growing up in Ohio, Jen Jones spent seven years as a cheerleader for her grade-school and high-school squads. Following high school, she coached several cheer squads to team victory. For two years, she also cheered and created dance numbers for the Chicago Lawmen semi-professional football dance team.

Jen gets her love of cheerleading honestly, because her mother, sister, and cousins are also heavily involved in the sport. As well as teaching occasional dance and cheerleading workshops, Jen now works in sunny Los Angeles as a freelance writer for publications like *American Cheerleader* and *Dance Spirit*.

Index